Dedication

This book is dedicated to the Holy Spirit for His inspiration

and to all the singles and married.

Contents

PRINCIPLES FOR A HAPPY MARRIED LIFE

Are you single or married? This book is for you!

For I know the plans I have for you, says the Lord.

They are plans for good and not for disaster,

To give you a future and a hope. Jeremiah 29:11

Charity Nnamoko

Unless otherwise indicated, all Scripture quotations are from the New King James Version and the New Living Translation Version of the Bible.

PRINCIPLES FOR A HAPPY MARRIED LIFE

ISBN: 978 969 2293 70 9

Acknowledgment

My appreciation goes to my husband Ken for all his support, suggestions, and the number of times he proofread the manuscript. Thank God for all the other people who helped make my writing dream a reality – the editor and the publishers.

Introduction

Marriage is a significant relationship that has a lot to do with the state of things on earth, and God is interested in it, so is the devil. Making sure your marriage is solidified at the onset is very important.

Most of the divorce cases you see today result from the wrong foundation in marriage and the enemy's plan to attack the union of marriage that God instituted. Young people go into marriage without knowing what the relationship involves or that you are supposed to be committed to the relationship, giving it a hundred percent commitment.

Some Christians also get into a marriage with unbelievers being ignorant of the consequences of such action.

As a young person raised by a single parent, you might wonder why there is so much divorce in marriages and much cheating among couples that are still together? Why no one respects the sanctity of the home and their body? Why is it that most youth no longer remain virgins until marriage? The answer is that the Jezebel spirit is responsible for adulterous and immoral acts today in the world and making many responsible women find it challenging to submit themselves to their husbands. Some women want to be the head contrary to the Word of God. 1 Peter 3:1 admonishes wives to "accept the authority of your husbands." Greed also pushes men into desiring other women besides their wives, and some go to the extent of seducing their friend's or brother's wives to have carnal knowledge of them, to name but a few. This Jezebel spirit is entirely in control of large parts of the world and gets hold of anyone that crosses her path. God warned us in the Scripture about her in Proverbs 5:3-10 "For the lips of an immoral woman are as sweet as honey, and her mouth is smoother than oil. But in the end, she is as bitter as poison, as dangerous as a double-edged sword." She is responsible for all the sexual abominations in the world today, and many Christians, even Pastors, are falling into her trap.

As a Christian, you have the power of God in you to enable you to overcome the enticement of this Jezebel spirit in your home, workplace, and ministry. Proverbs 1:10 "My child, if sinners entice you, turn your back on them!"

First, you must make the decision never to subject or yield your members to her by getting yourself involved in pre-marital sex. Never leave your partner for another woman or man who gives you sexual satisfaction or makes promises to you and cheat on your spouse while you are still living together.

This book contains a well of knowledge to get you equipped for your marriage.

Chapter One

Wisdom is the principal thing; therefore, get wisdom: and with all thy getting get understanding. Proverbs 4:7

Marry a Believer

Marriage is a Holy and Sacred relationship made by God, which is supposed to be unbroken, the same way you should not break your relationship with God. Getting married to a non-Christian or an unbelieving person means setting up a wrong foundation for your marriage. The tendency of the marriage ending up in divorce is high because you two have conflicting beliefs.

Don't team up with those who are unbelievers. How can righteousness be a partner with wickedness? How can light live with darkness? What harmony can there be between Christ and the devil? How can a believer be a partner with an unbeliever? And what union can there be between God's temple and idols? For we are the temple of the living God. As

God said: "I will live in them and walk among them. I will be their God, and they will be my people." (2 Corinthians 6:14-15).

Abstain from all appearance of evil. 1 Thessalonians 5:22.

When you choose an unbelieving person as your wife or husband, you are not abstaining from the appearance of evil, but rather with open arms welcoming several threats to your marriage and faith in God. I believe that God gave you all the principles needed to make the right decision regarding your marriage and enjoy it to the full, but the choice is yours, depending on your goal in life.

I heard of a case of a Christian that got married to an unbeliever with the hope to change the person (Note: It is not in your power to change anyone, including your partner, it is solely the job of the Holy Spirit), but the reverse was the case. The unbelieving partner stopped the wife from going to Church, visiting other Christians at home, praying, or reading the Bible at home. She made a mistake, and it cost her the happy marriage, she constantly desired to have. Today you can learn from the mistakes of other people and make a choice you will appreciate. God's desire for you is to be happy when married and enjoy the union and not the opposite.

Marriage is not a relationship you rush into because it is for life or until death separates you. It needs prayers and possibly fasting to hear from God before you make the decision. The answer could come in different forms, like having peace about the proposal, the person, a Scripture verse, or a dream. Wait patiently for the response in whichever way it will come.

My story – after Ken proposed to me, I asked him to give me some time to pray about it. I fasted and prayed about it. I received my answer in two ways; first was the peace of God, and secondly, from a stranger (an Evangelist). We invited an Evangelist to come and preach in our youth program, and at the end of the program, he asked us to form a circle and hold hands together. He stepped into the middle of the group and started prophesying over each one. I was excited to hear what God would say to me through the evangelist because, through him, God told some of the youths beautiful things about their future, His calling in their lives, and His plans for them. I was expecting something in the line of His calling and His plans. But when he got to me, he stood and just looked at me for a while and started telling me about the man God had set aside for me to marry, to confirm the answer I received earlier (inward peace).

Some Scriptures to help you as you make this critical decision:

1 Corinthians 15:13 "Be not deceived: evil communications corrupt good manners."

Proverbs 27:17 "As iron sharpens iron, so one person sharpens another."

1 Corinthians 10:31 "So whether you eat or drink, or whatever you do, do it all for the glory of God."

Your marriage should bring glory to God because He instituted the union of marriage and want those participating in this union to enjoy it to the fullest because the gift of God does not bring sorrow but will help you prosper even in your marriage.

Proverbs 3:5-6 (NIV)

5. *Trust in the Lord with all your heart and lean not on your own understanding.*

6. *In all your ways, submit to him, and he will make your paths straight."*

1   King 11:4-6 (NIV)

4. *"As Solomon grew old, his wives turned his heart after other gods, and his heart was not fully devoted to the Lord his God, as the heart of David his father had been.*

5. *He followed Ashtoreth, the goddess of the Sidonians, and Molek, the detestable God of the Ammonites.*

6. *So Solomon did evil in the eyes of the Lord; he did not follow the Lord completely, as David his father had done.*

Genesis 24: 2-4

2. *One day, Abraham said to his oldest servant, the man in charge of his household, "take an oath by putting your hand under my thigh.*

3. *Swear by the Lord, the God of heaven and earth, that you will not allow my son to marry one of these local Canaanite women.*

4. *Go instead to my homeland, to my relatives, and find a wife there for my son Isaac."*

Abraham understood the importance of ensuring that his son marries a believer and not any Canaanite women who worship other gods. Isaac was a covenant child, and God planned to fulfill some of His promises to Abraham through his son. Isaac choosing the wrong wife will affect the fulfillment of that promise. Let me bring it down to today. You are a covenant child of God, purchased with the precious blood of Jesus. Jesus paid the price for you to be His, and many promises are attached to the covenant, which you could easily miss by making the wrong choice in your marriage.

Chapter Two

Run from sexual sin! No other sin so clearly affects the body

As this one does. For sexual immorality is a sin against

Your own body. 1 Corinthians 6: 18.

Dating and Pre-marital sex

Have you wondered why many people date for five years or more and marry for just one year, and divorce? Some decide to live together and forget about the wedding. In most cases, they bear children outside wedlock, and when they finally decide to wed, the marriage lasts only for a few years, and they say goodbye?

I remembered discussing with a young girl who lives with her boyfriend; she said, "they are not planning to get married any sooner because she does not know yet if he is the right man for her." He is the right man for her to live with without marriage and might not be the right man for marriage. That is a big deception we see today in our society. You do not have to live with a man or woman before you know if you two can be husband and wife.

When you date, and sometimes you have sex and, in most cases, move in together, how do you want the young man to hurry up and marry you since he is enjoying what he should enjoy only after the wedding with you? You cook for him, go out for dinner, wash & iron his clothes, satisfy him sexually and even have a baby for him.

Hebrews 13:4 "Marriage is to be held in honor among all, and the marriage bed is to be undefiled; for fornicators and adulterers God will judge."

The above scripture passage shows that God does not support living with someone you are not married to because it does not help your marriage but rather it is a recipe for divorce. That means you are already sowing a bad seed into your marriage even before your wedding. Also, knowing that the devil hates marriage, he is responsible for single people not bothering about a wedding, but instead living together and enjoying what they should relish after marriage. As a result, when they finally decide to wed, the devil ensures the marriage never lasts. Hey! It is time we open our eyes and understand the tricks of the enemy and stop following them.

If someone says I love you and would like to marry you, but first we need to date for years, or you can move in with me, and we live together and see how it goes before we plan our wedding. Please kindly say this to the person, "I love you too, but I cannot share my love with you without a wedding ring." As a Christian youth or a single person, you can make a difference in this society; make it easy for people to distinguish between a believer and someone who does not honestly believe in God.

"For this is the will of God, your sanctification: that you abstain from sexual immorality; that each one of you knows how to control his own body in holiness and honor, not in the passion of lust like the Gentiles who do not know God."

1 Thessalonians 4:3-5 (ESV).

One thing about a sexual act that many people are unaware of is being a soul tier. It neats the soul of the two people involved together, at which point a covenant gets established. So, if you had a relation with 1, 2, 3, or more men or women before marriage, you have existing covenants with them that you need to break so that you will be free from the soul tier and only have one covenant with your married partner.

Flee from sexual immorality. Every other sin a person commits is outside the body, but the sexually immoral person sins against his own body. Or do you not know that your body is a temple of the Holy Spirit within you, whom you have from God? You are not your own, for you were bought with a price. So, glorify God in your body. 1Corinthians 6:18-20 (ESV)

Flee from any person who wants to have carnal knowledge of you before the wedding or even a married person who might try to seduce you and take advantage of you before you go into marriage. Remember all that glitter is not gold; sometimes the out is not as sweet as the act. You might end up being pregnant; the man rejects the pregnancy or advises you to go for an abortion or send you into the street; at that point, you will forget all that you experienced during the action.

Presently, I know it is a big challenge for young people and those not yet married to avoid temptation because the world sees it as a regular thing and not a big deal. The novels, movies, and even some publications in circulation are not helping matters at all. But remember that the grace of God is there for you to overcome any temptation that might come your way.

Here are more scriptures to read.

1 Corinthians 7:1-4

1. *Now for the matters, you wrote about: it is good for a man not to have sexual relations with a woman.*

2. *But since sexual immorality is occurring, each man should have sexual relations with his own wife, and each woman with her own husband.*

Romans 12: 1-2

1. *And so, dear brothers and sisters, I plead with you to give your bodies to God because of all he has done for you. Let them be a living and holy sacrifice – the kind he will find acceptable. This is truly the way to worship him.*

2. *Don't copy the behavior and customs of this world, but let God transform you into a new person by changing the way you think. Then you will learn to know God's will for you, which is good and pleasing and perfect.*

16

Chapter Three

Then the Lord said, "it is not good for the man to be alone; I will make him a helper suitable for him. Genesis 2:18

Knowing Each Other's Position

In marriage, each person has a responsibility. The woman is supposed to be a helper to her partner, to help him fulfill God's purpose for his life and at the same time realize her purpose. We will look at some of the commitments in the Bible.

Many ladies today still find it difficult to understand or accept their husband's position as the head of the family. Every organization chart is fundamental; it enables everyone to know their position and expectations. The organizational chart starts from The CEO (Chief Executive Officer) and goes down to the lowest level. It is a pity that this has been one of the chief causes of the crisis in the home. When everyone dictates what should take place, the couple will find it hard to reach an agreement. Knowing each other's position in the family is not supposed to cause any problem if you give yourselves to study the Word and understand God's mind concerning your marriage. I guess that is why the Bible says, "my people perish for lack of knowledge." Hosea 4:6. Satan uses the area of your ignorance to attack you. That is why the scriptures, Proverbs 3:5 state, "in all your getting get wisdom." You need Godly wisdom to be able to build your home the way God desires it to be. Let's look at a few of the commands given to couples to help each know their position and respect each other's role in the home.

Husband and Wife

Ephesians 5:21, 31-33

1. *And further, submit to one another out of reverence for Christ.*

31. *As the Scriptures say, "A man leaves his father and mother and is joined to his wife, and the two are united into one."*

32. *This is a great mystery, but it is an illustration of the way Christ, and the Church is one.*

33. *So again, I say, each man must love his wife as he loves himself, and the wife must respect her husband.*

Matthew 19:6

6 *Since they are no longer two but one, let no one split apart what God has joined together."*

It is the responsibility of husband and wife to guard their marriage jealously against all forces that would try to break them apart, including themselves.

Wives

Ephesians 5:22-24

22. *For wives, this means submit to your husbands as to the Lord.*

23. *For a husband is the head of his wife as Christ is the head of the Church. He is the Savior of his body, the Church.*

24. *As the Church submits to Christ, so you wives should submit to your husbands in everything.*

Ephesians 5: 33b

33b "and let the wife see that she respects her husband."

Colossians 3: 18-19

18. Wives, submit to your husband, as is fitting for those who belong to the Lord.

As a wife, you need to see your position and your obligations as your duties to God, not just for your husband. You are obeying the Lord as you submit to your husband. God made you a good home builder through God's wisdom because you need God to build your home the way He wants it to be. You might think that your role (submitting) is humiliating or difficult but look at the responsibilities God gave the man towards his wife. God expects the man to give his life to save his wife. Jesus did the same for His bride (the Church).

Husband

Ephesians 5:23, 25, 28, 33a

23. "For a husband is the head of his wife as Christ is head of the Church. He is the Savior of the body, the Church.

25. For husbands, this means love your wives, just as Christ loved the Church. He gave up his life for her.

28. In the same way, husbands ought to love their wives as their bodies. For a man who loves his wife actually shows love for himself.

33a. Nevertheless, let each one of you in particular so love his wife as himself.

1   Peter 3:7 (NLT)

7.   In the same way, you husbands must give honor to your wives. Treat your wife with understanding as you live together. She may be weaker than you are, but she is your equal partner in God's gift of new life. Treat her as you should so your prayers will not be hindered.

1   Corinthians 11:3 (NLT)

3. *But there is one thing I want you to know: The head of every man is Christ, the head of a woman is the man,*

4. *and the head of Christ is God.*

Colossians 3:19

19. *Husbands, love your wives and never treat them harshly.*

Note that being submissive to your husband does not make you inferior or less important than your husband. Remember that you are one; no one is greater than the other. "For this reason, a man shall leave his father and mother and be joined to his wife, and the two shall become one flesh. So then, they are no longer two, but one flesh. Therefore, what God has joined together, let not man separate" Matthew 19:5 (NKJV).

In Genesis 2:16-17, The Lord God commanded the man saying, "from any tree of the garden you may eat freely; but from the tree of the knowledge of good and evil you shall not eat, for in the day that you eat from it you will surely die." God looks at the man for the well-being of the family. He is the one God instructs on what should happen in his family. The family has its chart that moves from the man down to the kids or grandkids, just like you have an organizational chart in your office. Everyone mostly respects the boss happily without feeling inferior because you are an individual with lots of potentials, and God made you special and unique.

After God created Eve, He did not inform her about the tree of good and evil. God expected Adam to pass on the command to the wife and down to the kids. When Adam and Eve disobeyed God, He did not ask the woman what happened first, but the man, because God expected him to ensure that he and the wife obey God's command.

"For I have chosen him (Abraham), so that he may command his children and his household after him to keep the way of the Lord by doing righteousness and justice, so that the Lord may bring upon Abraham what He has spoken about him."

Genesis 18:19 (KJV).

God expects the man to ensure that his household keeps the way of the Lord and when he fails to do that, he will be the one to answer for that. Eli was unable to correct His children when they were doing wrong, and it cost his life and that of his sons 1 Samuel 3:11-14. Respecting each other's position in the home is very important and cannot be over-emphasized.

Chapter Four

Such love has no fear because perfect love expels all fear.

1 John 4: 18

Marry for love, and not out of pity

*L*ove and friendship should be the basis of your marriage and not pity. Never marry out of compassion. Marrying for love is very important because, in the event of misunderstanding or crises in your marriage, love will be the only thing that will hold you two together.

The following reasons are not enough to marry someone you plan to spend the rest of your life together with until death separates you. A) Marrying your best friend's fiancé after he passes away because you feel compassion for her. B) Wedding someone because they helped you out when in need, to pay the person back for the good they did for you. Do not let compassion be the reason you have to marry someone. What happens when you no longer pity the person or have long forgotten the incident that led to the marriage? Let peace and steadfast love with God as the foundation be your reason for getting married and not sympathy.

My Story: Before I got married, this young man attended the same fellowship with me. Sometimes he visited my local Church. It happened that we both wanted to marry each other because we had been helping each other. He helped me to prepare during my last High school exam. I helped him financially when he asked for it because I got a job while he received admission into the university. Deep down in my heart, I did not want to marry him because I could not withstand some characters of his. One of the things I have learned as a believer is that "God is always willing and ready to help you out of your confused state; all you need to do is ask Him.

One day I prayed for God to direct me and tell me what His will was concerning my marriage, and He made me understand that the guy I was considering getting married to is not the man He has for me. When the right man came, I knew deep down in my heart that he was the one because

I had peace within me. I accepted his proposal even though we didn't know each other before and did not live in the same country at that time. If you want your union to be the best, you must get God involved right from the onset so that He (the SOLID ROCK) will establish your marriage.

Points:

- You must pray and know the mind of God regarding your marriage.

- Check if you have the peace of God as you consider accepting the proposal or if you feel unsure and fearful?

- Are you comfortable with what you see – the character, faith level, etcetera?

- Check your heart and make sure you are not getting married out of sympathy or please someone else, maybe your parents or friends.

- If you feel peaceful and believe the Lord accepts the union, then go ahead.

- Be ready to be committed to your marriage and prayerfully give it 100% commitment, and you will live to enjoy it.

28

Chapter Five

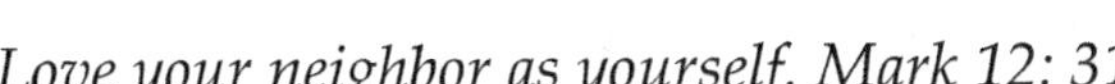

Love your neighbor as yourself. Mark 12: 31

Love Yourself

What picture of yourself do you see in your mind? Do you love yourself? Are there things you did in the past that made you hate yourself and find it hard to forgive yourself? Or derogatory and harmful words spoken over you by people? Do you see yourself as no good for any woman or man? Do you see yourself as a failure or disappointment? How you see yourself now will play many roles in your marriage and how your spouse will see you. "For as he thinketh in his heart, so is he" Proverbs 23:7a.

You are your thought, and your thought is you. You both are inseparable. You attract people that see you precisely the way you see and think about yourself. Remember, you are the landlord of your mind, so you can decide whom you rent space. Who do you currently rent space to in your life, and your thought? Do you rent it to bitterness, hopelessness, low self-esteem, loneliness, etcetera? Or are you renting the space to self-love, joy, peace, self-worth, hope, and thinking of yourself just the way God thinks of you?

Do not get into marriage if you don't love yourself because there is no way you will love your spouse if you don't love yourself. Real love flows from the inside, just as joy flows from the wells stored inside of you. "Love your neighbor as yourself." Romans 13:9. It is hard to love your neighbor the way you love yourself if you don't even love yourself. Remember, I am not talking about being self-centered, selfish, or only thinking about yourself. A self-centered person or selfish person always ends up having problems in their marriage. Marriage is a union that involves two people who are not selfish or think of themselves alone. Here, I am talking about having a positive attitude or testimony about you. How do you show that? How do you feel when you look at yourself in the mirror? How do you maintain your physical body, or do you eat yourself into obesity and various illnesses?

Psalm 19:14 states, "may these words of my mouth and this meditation of my heart be pleasing in your sight, LORD, my Rock, and my redeemer.

How do you feel or think of yourself when you see all your friends getting married and no one is approaching you for marriage? Do you think no one is coming to you because you are not pretty, or no lady is paying attention to you because you are not handsome or have no money? These are all the issues you need to deal with before going into marriage. Many people refuse to get married, and some end their marriage in divorce without dealing with the root cause.

You can ask God to help you love yourself before you go into marriage. If you are already married and struggling with a lack of love for yourself, I suggest you follow these steps, and I trust God will help you start loving yourself so that you can extend the love not just to your spouse alone but to others around you.

a) Take some time and ponder or remember what made you not love yourself (the incident).

b) Take that incident/case to God. He is your loving father. Tell Him the way you feel; if you need to cry, do that. It helps relieve the burden, and remember you have your Daddy's shoulder to cry on.

c) If you need forgiveness, ask your Heavenly Father, who is willing to forgive all your sins and to cleanse you from all unrighteousness. You can also ask forgiveness of someone involved if you believe you should do so. 1 John 1:9 "But if we confess our sins to Him, he is faithful and just to forgive us our sins and to cleanse us from all wickedness."

d) Forgive yourself and do not let the devil bring back guilt because you confessed, and God forgave you. 2 Corinthians 10:5b "bringing every thought into captivity to the obedience of Christ." Guilt is a dangerous weapon the devil uses against Christians. Watch your thoughts and pull down every idea that is contrary to God's Word.

e) Ask God to restore His love in you [you cannot love without God, because God is love] and heal your heart.

f) Go to the mirror, look at yourself and call yourself what your father calls you; a chosen race, a peculiar person, a royal priesthood, a unique person, the image of God and that you are fearfully and wonderfully made by God. 1 Peter 2:9, Genesis 1:26 and Psalm 139:14.

g) Now is an excellent opportunity to put your faith into action by confessing positive things with your mouth. Declare that you love yourself and that you are unique, you are fearfully and wonderfully made by God, that you are the image of God. You will receive what you confess. Romans 10:17, proverbs 18:20-21.

Ways to love yourself:

1. Proverbs 18:20 "Wise words satisfy like a good meal; the right words bring satisfaction." Always speak positive words about yourself, your looks, or your situation. Remember, life and death are in the power of your tongue, and you will receive what you speak, whether good or bad.

2. Take care of your body, what you put into your body, and the type of stress you assign to your body. Take time to relax your body, worry about nothing, and enjoy the rest and peace of God that is already available for you. 1 Peter 5:7 "Give all your worries and cares to God, for he cares about you."

3. Never accept negative words from people or allow them to dump their frustration or trashy words on you. Stay around positive people and the people that bring out the best in you.

4. Be happy and make laughter your second nature, even when you don't feel like it, because laughter is good medicine.

    Proverbs 17:22 A joyful heart is good medicine, but a crushed spirit dries up the bones.

    Job 8:21 He will yet fill your mouth with laughter and your lips with shouting.

    Proverbs 15:13 "A glad heart makes a cheerful face, but by sorrow of the heart, the spirit is crushed."

Psalm 126:2 Then our mouth was filled with laughter, and our tongue with shouts of joy; then they said among the nations, "The Lord has done great things for them."

Psalm 16:11 You make known to me the path of life; in your presence, there is fulness of joy; at your right hand are pleasures forevermore.

5. Always forgive because you are hurting yourself and opening doors to all kinds of diseases in your body when you do not forgive. Continuously tap into God's grace.

6. Learn to do something that gives you pleasure and something you are good at doing. Try to find your purpose because it will provide you with fulfillment. Like me, I love telling stories and encouraging people, using the scriptures, but I never have time to do that. I am always busy doing other things that do not give me as much pleasure as searching the scriptures and writing. But I decided to change that the same way I am encouraging you in this book to do.

7. Give yourself some credit and pat yourself on the back when you achieve a targeted goal, even when others see it as nothing significant. Look at yourself in the mirror and smile at the face you see and say nice words to yourself.

Chapter Six

Therefore, a man shall leave his father and mother and hold fast to his wife, and the two shall become one flesh.

Ephesians 5:31

Commitment

Commitments are all the efforts you put in to nurture your marriage relationship after making vows to each other. For your marriage to be enjoyable and satisfying, which is God's desire for your union, you need to be committed to it.

You should be committed 100 percent to your marriage, not 50 percent, and the other 50 percent to your extended family. Once married, your husband or wife is your immediate family – you two are one now. Your relationship with your spouse comes first; all the other connections are secondary. You can't claim you are committed to your marriage if you don't support each other; you can't miss your husband's graduation to attend your parent's birthday party. They are still your parents, but your commitment should be in your marriage and your spouse first.

Many people go into marriage with different ideas. Some go in with a heart made up to leave the spouse once they become unfaithful. It would help if you went into union to make it work and make your marriage heaven on earth. It is possible because the Bible said, "you can do all things through Christ, who strengthens you" (Philippians 4:13). If Christ is indeed your strength and you have a heart made up to make your marriage perfect, then you can achieve that as you commit yourself to it.

Some single and even married couples get tricked by some of the articles they read on marriage. Some magazine articles make us believe our union can be significant even when we are not committed to it. Other articles or movies portray things we will gain in our marriage, but not contribute to the union. Some people who write these articles share it from their own experiences or what they heard or read about someone else's experience. The truth is that you will not know all you need to know about marriage via those articles; in marriage, your own experience is your best teacher. I do not mean that you cannot study to educate yourself about it before entering a marriage. Of course, it is good you do so, but you must not expect your union to be like the one you read from the articles or expect your spouse to treat you the way these articles portray it.

You must go to God and ask that His perfect will for your marriage come to pass. Also, ask God to show you those areas you need to contribute to making your marriage work out well for both of you.

To enjoy your marriage, you must show some commitment, such as praying for your spouse, the union, and children. You must provide for your family, do things that will make your spouse happy, satisfy each other sexually. Also, you need to encourage and cheer up each other when the going gets tough and speak about what you want in your home. There is power in the spoken word. Life and death are in the power of your tongue. Even when circumstances prove otherwise, keep pressing on by praying and sowing good seeds into your marriage. Keep trusting God to bring His perfect will for your marriage to pass, which is for you to enjoy your union, spouse, and children if you have kids.

Some people say you need to commit 50% to your marriage while your spouse commits the other 50%. No, in marriage, the commitment level is 100% from each spouse. That means you have no reservations; you are committing all you are and all you have for your marriage, not keeping back 50%. Commitment brings about the continued growth of your marriage relationship and of both spouses. One important point to note in being committed to your marriage is making sure you keep your promises. If you promise to take her out for dinner, don't fail to do it. Another point is that you must not give room to outside forces to cause any problem in your marriage that will divide you. Always remain faithful to your partner and never cheat on them.

Commitment is not an easy task; it will always cost you something, the same way as athletes. They go through a lot to achieve what they want (winning their race and getting medals). But the end of it is always better because you will be the one enjoying it.

Knowing and accepting your responsibilities in marriage, as noted in the Bible, will make committing to your marriage easier.

Chapter Seven

Trust in the Lord with all your heart; do not depend on your own understanding. Proverbs 3: 5

It is not in your power to change your spouse

Never go into marriage with someone you know you cannot live with or someone you don't like their character with the view to change them. You don't go into marriage to change your partner because that will be the beginning of trouble; instead, you go into marriage to bring the best out of your partner. If you must marry the person, then don't think of changing them, but rather commit them into the hands of God and ask the Holy Spirit to change that area of their life the way He wants it to be. Do you know why I said the way He wants it to be? Because that thing you do not like in the person might be what God put in them to make them unique.

Let me give an example of two couples I know. The husband likes to be friendly, talks to people (neighbors), laughs always. The wife is quiet, doesn't like talking to strangers, except close friends and family, and often doesn't respond to greetings. Most times, she gets angry when they get back, and the husband stops to say hi to their neighbor, and she walks past them without saying a word to the neighbor. She can't change the spouse's outgoing nature. I don't think God will be willing to change that with him because He wants us to be friendly to people, not just our close friends or family. (Love your neighbor as yourself - Mark 12:31). So, if you can't stand a person with such character, then do not marry the person because you will be setting a wrong foundation for your marriage. After all, you could wake up one day and decide to call it quits and look for someone with the kind of character you admire.

You can avoid going through divorce by making the right choice from the beginning. Remember, marriage is not a vacation; it is a lifetime affair, so you must make a calculated and prayerful decision that will enable you to experience a blissful marriage that will stand all tests, even divorce. Let me give one more example. I heard of two people that got married; meanwhile, before they got married, the man said, oh, now that I've found my wife, you will be helping me arrange things; I am not an organized person. She said, oh! No problem, I will teach you how to set things. A few months after their wedding, she tried without any success to help him learn how to hang his pant and shirt, put his shoes in the closet, put trash in the trash bin. He places them anywhere convenient for him, not really where they are supposed to be. And one day, when she could not stand it any longer, she left him.

Today I hear many single people say, I like this person, but I am not too fond of this aspect of their character. Note that no one has a perfect personality; some have good traits that need to be developed by their partner. In marriage, you will have to bring out the best in each other. Like I mentioned earlier if you must marry the person, don't plan to change them, but rather concentrate on bringing out the best in them. You might end up seeing that area of their life you don't like change.

Before I got married, I wasn't the friendly type; what makes others happy annoys me sometimes. Before we got married, I told Ken that I was not used to laughing and smiling in pictures; he didn't run away. He didn't try to change me but instead concentrated on bringing out the best in me. Today I am more friendly and laugh more than he does (laughs, just kidding). We both are friendly and happy, something I never thought I could do. Spouses bringing out the best in each other is one of the numerous benefits of marriage, and you can achieve that through prayers and allowing God to do the work for you.

Chapter Eight

A word fitly spoken is like apples of gold in a setting of silver.

Proverbs 25: 11

Talk Things Over - Communicate

Before marriage, I advise that you talk things over. Like each other's idea of marriage, how many kids you plan to have, your likes, dislikes, and your calling or ministry. Surprisingly, these unresolved issues also contribute to the crisis in the home that, in some cases, end up in divorce.

Most young people do not see communication as an essential ingredient that will help them even when married. Couples getting to know each other are always eager to agree with what the other suggests without thinking. Even when the other partner makes known their desire not to have a baby or raise a family, if you are interested in having a family, you should not marry someone who is not interested in doing so. Some of these unions end in divorce, and the spouse that wants to have children will get married to someone interested in having children.

It would help to discuss finances. Do you need to know each other's views on having a joint account and understanding each other's earning? Make sure they are not the greedy type that will do anything for money or just get into the marriage for money. Find out each other's strengths in handling finances. One partner could be a good saver and the other a spender, which will help you decide who is better suited to handle the families' finances.

You can also plan for when you have children. Will one of the spouses stay home, or should your child go to daycare until school age? Should one be working or one staying home when you have kids? I know some men want their wives to stay home while they work and take care of the family, but it could pose a problem if your partner likes their career and wants to be in the workforce. If you talk about these topics before tying the knot, it closes different avenues through which the devil would have stepped into your marriage.

Talking things over does not end when you are married. Communication is one of the pillars that holds any marriage together. Once you stop communicating with your spouse, you open the door to secrets, resentment, lack of trust, and distance from each other. Just like a plant needs water to grow, so is your marriage with communication. You can build each other up, bring out the best and encourage each other to overcome your fears through communication. Most marital crises can be resolved through communication, talking things over.

Getting wisdom is the wisest thing you can do! And whatever else you do, develop good judgement.

Proverbs 4:7 (NLT)

Chapter Nine

Therefore, a man shall leave his father and mother and hold fast

to his wife, and the two shall become one flesh.

Ephesians 5:31

Be Faithful To Each Other

You ought to make up your mind before marriage not to cheat on your partner and don't cease to ask God for His grace to flee from every trace of sin or evil. You can't avoid it by your power or how spiritual or intelligent you are. It does not take a philosophical or spiritual person from running away from immoral sin, but one who depends on the grace of God to help them overcome every situation.

The Bible contains advice and ways to avoid this temptation and the consequences of indulging in this sin.

8. [Let your way of life be far from her, and come not near the door of her house [avoid the very scenes of temptation].

9. [Lest you give your honor to others and your years to those without mercy.

10. [Lest strangers [and false teachers] take their fill of your strength and wealth and your labors to go to the house of an alien [from God]

15. [Drink waters out of your cistern [of a pure marriage relationship], and fresh running waters out of your well.

16. Should your offspring be dispersed abroad as water-brooks in the streets?

17. [Confine yourself to your wife] let your children be for you alone, and not the children of strangers with you.

18. Let your fountain [of human life] be blessed [with the rewards of fidelity] and rejoice in the wife of your youth.

19. Let her be as the loving hind and pleasant doe [tender, gentle, attractive] --let her bosom satisfy you at all

times, and always be transported with delight in her love.

20. Why should you, my son, be infatuated with a loose woman, embrace the bosom of an outsider, and go astray?

21. For the ways of man are directly before the eyes of the Lord, and He [Who would have us live soberly, chastely, and godly] carefully weighs all man's goings.

Destroy every evil thought the devil might have sown in you because of what you experienced in your first marriage or between your parents. Break off every link of unfaithfulness in marriage if any of your parents practiced it. Why? Because the devil takes pleasure in seeing that any bad thing done by parents goes down generations. That is why we see many Christians being diagnosed with diseases that their parents suffered, and some whose parents divorced when they were young, in some cases, end up divorcing their partner when they get married. I advise you to detach yourself from anything that runs in your family, which you don't like, for example, sickness, divorce, unfaithfulness in marriage, poverty, etcetera.

Some people who have a marital crisis are due to the forces working against them from previous generations. The earlier you get your marriage cleaned of all these things, the better for both couples.

Ensure that you stick to your wife or husband alone and don't lust after another woman or man.

Proverbs 6:25-29 (AMP)

25. *Lust not after her beauty in your heart, neither let her capture you with her eyelids.*

26. *For on account of a harlot, a man is brought to a piece of bread, and the adulteress stalks and snares [as with a hook] the precious life [of a man].*

27. *Can a man take fire in his bosom, and his clothes not be burned?*

28. *Can one go upon hot coals, and his feet not be burned?*

29. *So, he who cohabits with his neighbor's wife [will be tortured with evil consequences and just retribution]; he who touches her shall not be innocent or go unpunished.*

James 4:7 "So be subject to God. Resist the devil [stand firm against him], and he will flee from you" (AMP).

It is surprising that with all the resources available to us (the Bible) and the grace of God, which abounds with us, many Christians still fall into the hands of the strange woman or man.

Try not to quench the romance in your marriage because it helps keep the marriage going at a time of crisis in your marriage and will help resolve issues that arise in the home faster. Don't stay too long without making love to your spouse, and don't deny each other that pleasure; such could lead your spouse to find somewhere to satisfy themselves outside the home.

Do not refuse and deprive and defraud each other [of your due marital right], except perhaps by mutual consent for a time so that you may devote yourselves unhindered to prayer. But afterward, resume marital relations, lest Satan tempts you [to sin] through your lack of restraint of sexual desire. I Corinthians 7:5 (AMP)

Chapter Ten

Praying always with all prayer and supplication in the spirit.

Ephesians 6:18

Pray for One Another and Your Marriage

Do you believe your marriage is worth your prayers? Do you think prayer works even in marriage? Is it a sacrifice you will be willing to make when you get married? Because you will face challenges from within and outside of your union. Challenges can arise because you are two unique individuals with different personalities, interests, and strengths living together. You could face challenges from relatives who want to run your marriage or family members that will not accept you into the family or just outrightly show their hatred towards you for no fault of yours.

Marriage is not always 100% crisis-free. Many times, trials come to test the faith of your union. During a marital problem is a good time to measure how strong your marriage is, 10%, 30%, 50%, 60%, how mature you have become over time by living with a stranger who turned out to be your best friend, lover, helper, encourager, etcetera.

Do not cease to commit your marriage always into God's hands, for Him to preserve it. "Pray without ceasing" (Thessalonians 5:17).

It is not too early to start declaring what you want in your marriage. Set the foundation spiritually through prayers, sowing seeds of faith, and studying the scriptures to prepare you. You can begin now to fast and pray for your marriage, do not wait until you are married to start. I have been married for 18 years, but I started praying for my marriage when I was single. I prayed for the kind of man I wanted God to bless me. I sowed financial seeds with prayer points of what I wanted in my marriage. I can tell you that God answered my prayers and gave me more than what I asked of Him. And He can do the same for you because He loves you and wants the best for you.

Praying for your marriage is not a choice but a requirement for a victorious marriage made in heaven.

1 Thessalonians 5:16-18

16. Rejoice always

17. Pray without ceasing,

18. Give thanks in all circumstances, for this is the will of God in Christ Jesus for you.

The will of God is that you rejoice always. Pray without ceasing for your marriage and thank God for your spouse, yourself, and your unification.

The Way of Love

1 Corinthians 13 will help you learn how to love yourself and your spouse. When you encounter any problem in your marriage, remember that following the way of love will restore and heal your marriage. Read this Scripture prayerfully, and let the Holy Spirit guide and help you.

1 Corinthians 13: 1-8, 9

1. If I could speak all the languages of earth and of angels but didn't love others, I would only be a noisy gong or a clanging cymbal.

2. If I had the gift of prophecy, and if I understood all of God's secret plans and possessed all knowledge, and if I had such faith that I could move mountains but didn't love others, I would be nothing.

3. If I gave everything I have to the poor and even sacrificed my body, I could boast about it; but if I didn't love others, I would have gained nothing.

4. Love is patient and kind. Love is not jealous or boastful or proud

5. Or rude. It does not demand its own way. It is not irritable, and it keeps no record of being wronged.

6. It does not rejoice about injustice but rejoices whenever the truth wins out.

7. Love never gives up, never loses faith, is always hopeful, and endures through every circumstance.

8. Prophecy and speaking in unknown languages and special knowledge will become useless. But love will last forever!

13. Three things will last forever – faith, hope, and love – and the greatest of these is love.

A list of the qualities you want in your husband or wife

Prayers for your marriage